SPEEDY SCIENCE

Edited by Angela Royston

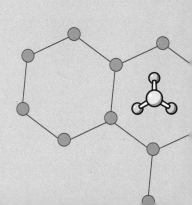

W

FRANKLIN WATTS

LONDON • SYDNEY

First published in 2014
by Franklin Watts

Copyright © Franklin Watts 2014

Franklin Watts
338 Euston Road
London NW1 3BH

Franklin Watts Australia
Level 17/207 Kent Street
Sydney, NSW 2000

Editor: Sarah Peutrill
Designer: Jason Anscomb

Photos © Franklin Watts, apart from: 17t Pablo Eder/Shutterstock; 18t and 19t; Scott Rothstein/Shutterstock. 18mr: Home Studio/Shutterstock; 18ml Nigel Cattlin FLPA; 19: Brush, Adam Borkowski/Shutterstock. Pseudoscorpion, Cosmin Manci/Dreamstime. Hands, Shutterstock. 20: Spoon, Travis Klein/Shutterstock. Plastic glasses, Homestudio/Shutterstock. Washing hands, Shutterstock. 21: Plastic boxes, Scott Rothstein/Shutterstock. Magnifying glass, Shutterstock. Paintbrush, Adam Borkowski/Shutterstock. Seven-spot ladybird, Steve Shoup/Shutterstock. 79t: JPL/NASA.

These experiments previously appeared in the following books: Starting science series by Sally Hewit: *Animals, Human body, Plants*; Where to find minibeasts series by Sarah Ridley: *Under a stone, In the soil, In a pond, On a flower*; Investigating science series by Jacqui Bailey: *Why does light cast shadows?, What does a magnet do? How can solids be changed? How do we use electricity? How do we use materials?* One-stop science series by Angela Royston: *Experiments with a torch, Experiments with a lemon, Experiments with a ruler*; Science experiments series by Sally Nankivell-Aston and Dorothy Jackson: *Sound, Water, Electricity, Forces*; The real scientist series by Peter Riley: *Bang!, Space! Stuff!*

Every attempt has been made to clear copyright. Should there be any inadvertent omission please apply to the publisher for rectification.

Dewey number: 507.8
HB ISBN: 978 1 4451 2929 7
Library ebook ISBN: 978 1 4451 2930 3

Printed in China

Franklin Watts is a division of Hachette Children's Books, an Hachette UK company.
www.hachette.co.uk

CONTENTS

THINK LIKE A SCIENTIST!

Scientists are fascinated and curious about the world around them. They want to understand how everything works, from the simplest to the most complicated things. They ask questions and try to find the answers.

PRACTICAL ANSWERS

When scientists ask questions about the world, they are looking for answers based on facts. They design experiments to discover new facts and to test their ideas. They compare what happens in different situations and they look for patterns. If they do not get the answer they expect, they try to understand what happened and why. Did they do something wrong or was their idea wrong?

REAL SCIENCE

You can be a scientist too! This book is full of experiments that you can do at home or in the classroom. Before you start the experiments, read how to work like a scientist (pages 6 and 7). This book has been designed to make things easier for you.

GETTING STARTED

The first paragraph tells you what the experiment is about. Before you begin the experiment, make sure you have all the stuff you need. Use the 'What do I need?' list to collect everything before you start.

HOW LONG WILL IT TAKE?

The clock symbol tells you how long the main part of the experiment is likely to take. You may take longer, or be quicker. The time does not include getting everything ready, or clearing up afterwards. Some experiments need to be checked every few hours or over several days. The time in between is not included.

WHAT HAPPENED?

When you do an experiment think about what happened and try to work out why. Then read 'What happened?' to see if you were right.

WARNING!

A warning sign tells you that you need to take special care. Some experiments need the help or presence of an adult. Always be careful if you are cutting or heating something.

WORK LIKE A SCIENTIST

Scientists carry out experiments carefully and methodically. They think about the experiment and predict what they think will happen. They make sure that the experiment is fair and they observe everything that happens. They then examine their results to see if their prediction was correct. You must do all of these things too!

PREDICT THE ANSWER

Make sure you are clear what the experiment is about and try to predict the result. Are you comparing different materials or situations? What do you think the outcome will be? Are you going to mix things together? What change do you expect to see? When you have completed the experiment, check to see if your prediction was correct.

A FAIR TEST

A fair test is an experiment that changes only one thing at a time. If you are comparing different things or situations, change only the thing you are testing. Make sure that you keep everything else the same. Some experiments include tips for keeping the test fair.

WATCH CAREFULLY

Observe everything that happens. If your experiment involves measuring the results, make sure you use rulers, scales, thermometers or other measuring devices correctly.

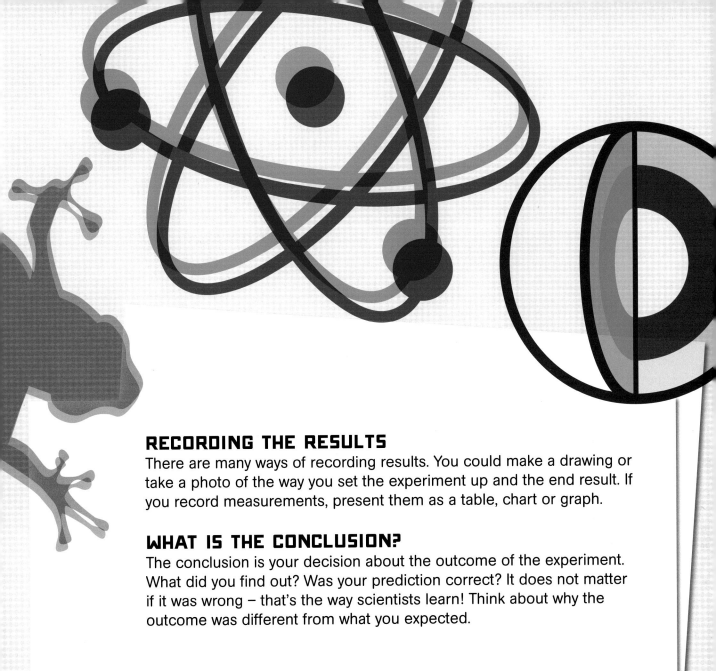

RECORDING THE RESULTS

There are many ways of recording results. You could make a drawing or take a photo of the way you set the experiment up and the end result. If you record measurements, present them as a table, chart or graph.

WHAT IS THE CONCLUSION?

The conclusion is your decision about the outcome of the experiment. What did you find out? Was your prediction correct? It does not matter if it was wrong – that's the way scientists learn! Think about why the outcome was different from what you expected.

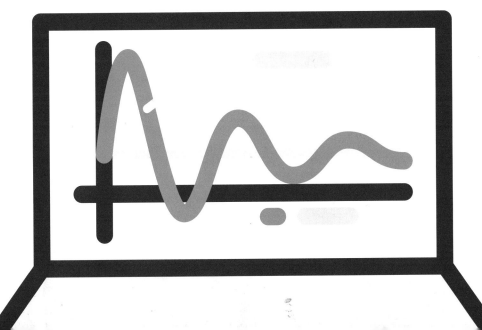

TURN PARTS OF A PLANT BLUE

10 mins

A plant has roots, a stalk, leaves, flowers and fruit. This experiment compares a root, a stalk and a flower to see if the water reaches them all. Which do you think will turn blue?

WHAT DO I NEED?

- 3 jars of water
- blue food colouring
- old carrot
- celery stalk with leaves
- white carnation
- paper
- crayons (or a camera)

2

WHAT DO I DO?

1. Put enough drops of food colouring in each jar to make the water a strong blue colour.

2. Put the carrot, the celery stalk and the carnation in the jars.

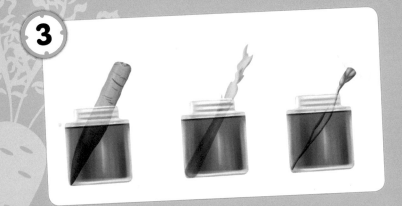

3

3. Draw the plant in each jar, copying the colours as accurately as you can (or take a photograph).

4. Look at the jars every few hours during the day and again the next day. Draw or photograph the changes you see. Record your findings on a chart. Did the carrot, the celery or the flower turn blue fastest? How long did it take?

WHAT HAPPENED?

Each plant part turns blue because water moves through tiny tubes inside the plant. It moves from the roots, through the stalk and even into the flower.

20 mins

PARTS OF A FLOWER

Colourful flowers have brightly coloured petals. Different species of flower look different, but do they have some things that are the same? This experiment pulls a flower apart to see what else makes up a flower.

WHAT DO I NEED?

- big flower with colourful, scented petals
- white card
- clear glue or clear sticky-backed plastic
- pencil or pen

WHAT DO I DO?

1. Carefully pull each petal off the flower. Count the petals and lay them out on the white card.

2. Pull off each stamen. Count them and lay them out on the card.

3. Remove the pistil and the ovary without separating them.

4. Write the name of the flower and label the parts.

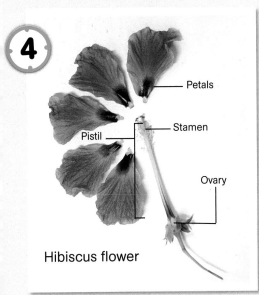

Petals
Stamen
Pistil
Ovary

Hibiscus flower

5. Cover the whole card with the sticky-backed plastic or spread glue on the card and lay the parts on top. You could also press a whole flower to include in your display.

6. Do this with several different types of flower. Compare the number of petals and stamens.

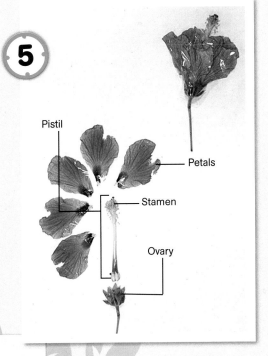

Pistil
Petals
Stamen
Ovary

WHAT HAPPENED?

All colourful flowers have petals, a pistil and stamens. The number of petals and stamens vary from one kind of flower to another.

30 mins

WHAT DO PLANTS NEED TO GROW?

Find out what plants need by testing whether they can grow without light, water or soil. Mung beans or geranium seeds work well in this experiment. Just scatter the seeds in damp compost and wait until they sprout into seedlings.

WHAT DO I NEED?

- 4 seedlings (geranium seedlings will work well) OR mung bean seeds
- potting soil
- small flower pots
- small watering can
- jar of water
- ruler or tape measure

Seedling	Day	Height	Comments
1 – soil, water, sunlight	12	6cm	taller and healthy looking
	15	6.5cm	2 new leaves
	18		
2 – soil, water, no sunlight	12	5cm	looking a bit pale
	15		
	18		
3 – soil, no water, sunlight	12	5cm	wilting slightly

WHAT DO I DO?

1. Give the first seedling all it needs to grow. Plant it in soil, put it in a sunny place and give it enough water to keep the soil moist.

2. Plant the second seedling, keep it watered but put it in a dark cupboard. Plant the third seedling, put it in a sunny place but don't water it. Put the fourth seedling in a jar of water in a sunny place.

3. Keep a record of how each seedling grows. Write your findings down on a chart.

4. Which seedling grows the best? Which seedling grows the worst? What conditions do the seedlings prefer? Why do you think that is?

5. You could repeat this experiment with seedlings of a different plant. Remember to wash your hands after you touch soil.

WHAT HAPPENED?

Plants need water and sunlight to grow, so only the first seedling should have grown well. Seedlings 2 and 3 would slowly die. Some seeds can grow in water only, others need soil to grow well.

5 mins

WATCH A SEED GROW

The whole of a plant – even a tree – starts off as a single seed. Follow this experiment to see what happens. How long do you think it will take for seedlings to grow?

WHAT DO I NEED?

- large, flat beans such as broad beans (or fava beans)
- glass jar
- kitchen towel (or cotton wool)
- paper
- ruler
- pencil and crayons
- flowers pots and soil

WHAT DO I DO?

1. Soak a few beans in water overnight.

Day	Picture of growth	Root/shoot measurement
1		0cm
4		2cm
7		Root 3.5cm/ shoot 1cm

2. Damp some kitchen towel right through with water. Use it to line the jar.

4. Leave the jar somewhere warm and light and make sure the kitchen towel is always damp. Keep a record of each new plant's growth. You could draw pictures, write comments and take measurements. Plant the seedlings in pots of soil when they start to grow leaves.

WHAT HAPPENED?

First a root grows out of the seed, and then a shoot. The root grows downward and the shoot grows up. Whichever way up you plant the seed, the same thing happens. Did your beans grow slower or faster than you expected?

3. Push the beans equal distances apart in between the jar and the damp kitchen towel.

FOOD CHAINS THAT INCLUDE YOU

30 mins

Every item of food you eat is part of a food chain. Some chains are short, others are longer. Without the links in the chain, you would have nothing to eat! Explore some of the food chains that end with you.

WHAT DO I NEED?

- large sheet of card
- pencils and crayons

WHAT DO I DO?

1. Write down some of the food you might eat for each meal in a day.

2. Make a list of the main ingredients. If the food is wrapped, the packaging will include a list of all the ingredients, with the main ingredient or ingredients first.

3. Draw a chart, like the one shown here, with the food in one column and a list of ingredients for each food.

4. Use books or the Internet to find the food chain for each ingredient. To do this, think about what the ingredient comes from and how it got its food. For example, an egg comes from a chicken. The chicken ate corn. Trace each ingredient back to a plant.

5. Add the food chain for each ingredient into the chart, starting with the plant and ending with you.

Breakfast	
Porridge	Oats/porridge – me
Boiled egg	Corn – chicken/egg – me
Lunch	
Cheese sandwich	Wheat/bread – me
	Grass – cow/butter – me
	Grass – cow/cheese – me
	Lettuce – me

WHAT HAPPENED?

All food chains begin with plants. That is because plants use the energy of sunlight to make their own food from water and carbon dioxide. Animals (including humans) eat other animals or plants.

WHOSE TEETH?

1 hour

WHAT DO I NEED?

- white card
- pencils and crayons
- scissors

Herbivores eat only plants, carnivores eat only meat and omnivores eat both. Animals (and humans) have different shapes of teeth depending on the type of food they eat. This is a game to play with a friend. It challenges you to match each animal to its teeth and its food.

WHAT DO I DO?

1. Cut the card into 18 equal rectangles. Using the table on the right as a guide, make six sets of three cards. Draw a picture or write a word on each card to show an animal, its teeth, and the group it belongs to – carnivore, omnivore or herbivore. Play the game with a friend. The first to collect two sets of three cards that go together is the winner!

2. Deal four cards each and place the remaining cards face down in a pile. Pick up one card from the pile, without showing it to your friend. Put a card you don't want face down, starting a new pile of cards.

3. Ask your friend to pick up a card from the first pile and put down a card on the second pile. When the first pile of cards has been used, start to use the second pile. Try to keep cards that will make up a set.

Picture	Picture	Word
Lion		Carnivore
Shark		Carnivore
Human		Omnivore
Gorilla		Omnivore
Sheep		Herbivore
Cow		Herbivore

4. As soon as one player has a set, lay them out and pick three more cards off the pile. Carry on until one player gets two complete sets and wins!

WHAT HAPPENED?

Large, flat teeth are good for chewing plants and sharp teeth slice into meat. Some animals have both.

MAKE A CROCODILE SKELETON

1 hour

A skeleton is all the bones in the body. Vertebrates are animals with backbones. They include mammals, birds and reptiles. This activity shows you how a crocodile's bones fit together to make the crocodile's shape. Ask an adult to help you with this activity.

WHAT DO I NEED?

- sheet of A3 white card
- pencil
- black pen
- scissors
- pin
- 6 paper fasteners

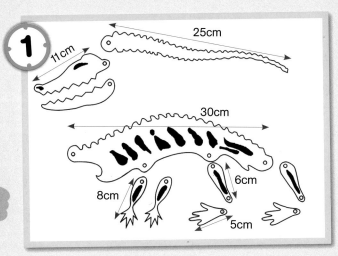

1

25cm

11cm

30cm

6cm

8cm

5cm

WHAT DO I DO?

1. On the white sheet of card, draw the templates shown above of the two parts of the crocodile skull, the body, the tail, the two front and two back legs, and the two back feet. Fill in the dark shapes with a black pen.

2. Cut out the templates. Ask an adult to use the pin to make small holes where the circles are marked. Push a paper fastener through the pin holes to make them bigger.

3. Fold back and forth along the sections of the tail as shown, as if you were making a fan, to make it moveable.

3

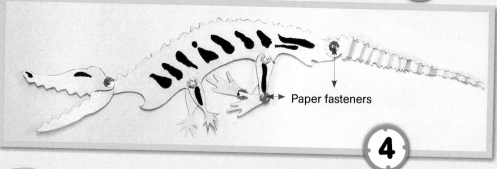

Paper fasteners

4

4. Join the skeleton parts together with paper fasteners where marked. Make sure each joint is loose enough for the parts to move. Watch the bones of your crocodile move as you walk it along!

WHAT HAPPENED?

The joints are the places where two bones meet. They allow the bones to move and so allow the crocodile to move.

30 mins

HOW STRONG IS A BONE?

Bones have to be strong to take your weight and allow you to do heavy work without breaking or collapsing. At the same time bones have to be light enough to move easily. This experiment shows how your bones are constructed to be strong but light.

WHAT DO I NEED?

- sheet of A4 coloured paper
- scissors
- sticky tape
- paperback books

WHAT DO I DO?

1. Cut two pieces of A4 paper into three pieces, lengthways, to get six strips of paper about 21cm x 10cm. Roll one strip into a short tube, and fix it with sticky tape.

2. Stand the tube upright on a flat surface. Place a book across the top of it. How many books will the tube hold before it collapses? Remake the tube if needed.

3. Cut the remaining paper strips lengthways to make smaller strips about 4cm x 10cm. Roll each one into a long tube and fix with sticky tape.

4. Pack the inside of the large tube with the smaller tubes standing upright. Test the tube for strength again. How many books can it support before it collapses this time?

WHAT HAPPENED?

The new tube is much stronger than the first one. Like a bone, it has a hard outside, with hollow tubes inside. The tubes strengthen the bone but keep it light.

30 mins

MAKING A MOVE

You need muscles and joints, as well as bones, to move. This game tests how strong your muscles are, how well your joints move and how good your balance is!

WHAT DO I DO?

1. Using the A4 card, cut four playing card-sized pieces of white card and four each of red, yellow, blue and green card.

2. Cut a circle about 28cm across from each piece of A3 coloured card.

3. On the white cards write:
i) right foot   ii) left foot
iii) right hand   iv) left hand.
Shuffle the white cards and put them face down in a pile. Shuffle the coloured cards and put them in a pile next to the white cards.

4. Player 1 stands on some grass, or a soft mat, with the four coloured circles around him or her. Player 2 picks up a white card (e.g. 'right hand'), then picks up a coloured card (e.g. 'green'). Player 1 puts their right hand on the green circle.

5. Player 2 calls out all the white cards, with a colour, and player 1 follows the instructions. Keep calling the cards until player 1 loses their balance and falls over! Then swop over. The winner is the player who can make the most moves without losing their balance.

WHAT HAPPENED?

Were you aware of moving different joints and muscles? Did you have to stretch, twist and shift your weight between your hands and feet?

SEE AND COUNT YOUR HEARTBEATS

10 mins

WHAT DO I NEED?
- blob of poster putty
- drinking straw
- timer

Your heart pumps blood around your body. The blood is pushed out of the heart and into your arteries. Every time your heart beats, the arteries bulge a little. You can feel this 'pulse' in the arteries in your wrist and neck. This experiment uses the pulse in your wrist to move a straw, and so makes it easy for you to count your pulse.

WHAT DO I DO?

1. Find the pulse in your wrist by feeling for it with the fingers of your other hand.

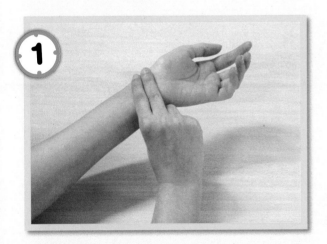

2. Push the blob of poster putty gently onto the spot where the pulse feels strongest, so it stays in place. Now push one end of the straw into the putty so it stands upright.

3. Lie your arm flat on a table and watch the straw twitch with each pulse beat. How many times does the straw twitch in one minute?

4. Take your pulse at different times of day. For example, when you have just woken up, after running upstairs or after a meal.

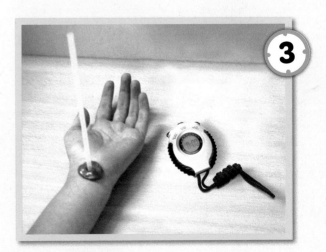

5. Make a chart of your results.

WHAT HAPPENED?

When you exercise, your body needs extra oxygen to supply your muscles, so your heart beats faster. When you are resting, your heart beats more slowly.

MAKE A
PITFALL TRAP

A habitat includes all the living things in a particular area. Many living things are hard to see because they live out of sight in the soil, or in the trees or bushes, in the water or under a stone. The next four experiments show you how you can collect animals in different habitats.

WHAT DO I DO?

1. Dig a hole big enough for your jam jar or container. Sink the container into the hole, so the rim is level with the soil.

WHAT DO I NEED?

- jam jar or plastic pot
- trowel or spade
- 4 small stones
- flat stone, piece of slate, bathroom tile or piece of Perspex

3. Leave the trap overnight and check it in the morning. Use an identification chart, website or book to identify your captives and then release them. Otherwise your minibeasts will die of hunger or eat each other!

4. Keep a record of what you trapped and count how many of each type of minibeast you captured. Draw or photograph each type.

5. Release the minibeasts. Remove the container and fill in the hole when you have finished.

2. Place a piece of Perspex or similar flat object on four stones around the container, forming a roof with a gap underneath it so that the minibeasts can fall in the trap. This will stop any rain from drowning the minibeasts.

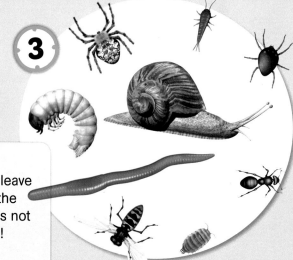

WHAT HAPPENED?

If your trap failed to catch many minibeasts, leave a bit more space between the Perspex and the ground. Make sure the rim of the container is not higher than the soil. Try again, the next night!

30 mins

A HANDFUL OF SOIL

You may be amazed to find what lives in the soil. What do you expect to find?

WHAT DO I NEED?

- large sheet of white paper
- disposable gloves
- handful of garden soil or leaves
- fine paintbrush
- collecting pots or tubs
- magnifying glass or microscope

WHAT DO I DO?

1. Lay the sheet of paper on a table. Wearing the gloves, fetch a handful of soil. Carefully tip the soil onto the white paper and spread it around.

2. Using the paintbrush, slowly move the soil around to look for minibeasts. Carefully lift the minibeasts into a collecting pot.

3. Use an identification chart, website or book to identify your minibeasts.

4. Remember to return the soil and the minibeasts to where you found them.

5. In the autumn, you could repeat the activity using a handful of leaves.

Wash your hands after you have handled soil and leaves.

40 mins

POND DIPPING

Lots of minibeasts live in a pond. You can collect them by pond dipping.

WHAT DO I NEED?

- strong net with a long handle
- plastic trays (e.g. large ice-cream cartons)
- plastic spoons or plastic cups
- magnifying glass

WHAT DO I DO?

1. Ask an adult to half fill your plastic collecting trays with pond water. Quickly sweep the net across the surface of the pond and then lower it into the collecting tray. Turn the net inside out to release the contents. Lift out the net. What have you found?

2. Now repeat the steps above but sweep the net under the water and empty the contents into a different plastic tray. Finally, let the net sink to the bottom of the pond and empty the net into a third collecting tray. Use a plastic spoon or cup to capture a minibeast for a closer look. A magnifying glass can give a new view of a really small creature. Use an identification chart, website or book to identify your minibeasts.

3. Take great care with minibeasts as it is easy to hurt them. Remember to return them all to the pond when you have finished.

⚠ Always go pond dipping with an adult. Wash your hands after you have been pond dipping and before you eat!

WHAT HAPPENED?

Some pond minibeasts live mostly at the top, middle or bottom of the pond, but others are found at different depths. For example, worms live in the mud on the bottom.

SHAKING THE BRANCHES

30 mins

Discover how many minibeasts are in a bush or a tree by following these instructions.

WHAT DO I NEED?

- big white bed sheet, or a large piece of white paper
- magnifying glass
- plastic containers for collecting minibeasts
- small paintbrush for gently moving minibeasts about

WHAT DO I DO?

1. Choose a bush or a tree and place the sheet or paper underneath it. Give the plant a good shake. If you are lucky, lots of tiny creatures will fall down onto your sheet or paper.

2. Carefully place some of the minibeasts in your containers for a closer look. You have to be very gentle with minibeasts as they are small animals that can easily be hurt. Use the paintbrush or a piece of grass or a twig to move them.

3. Use an identification chart, website or book to identify your minibeasts and then put them back in the branches of the bush or tree.

4. Keep a record of what you found and how many of each type of minibeast you counted. Draw or photograph each type.

WHAT HAPPENED?

Compare your results from different habitats (pages 18–21). Did you find any minibeast in more than one habitat? Some animals are suited to one particular type of habitat. Pond minibeasts are not likely to live outside water. Many of the other minibeasts may be found in several habitats, on plants or on the ground and even in the soil.

CAN YOU SEE IN THE DARK?

25 mins

WHAT DO I NEED?
- blindfold (e.g. a scarf)
- friend
- some small 'mystery' objects
- cake tin or a box with a lid

Light lets us see things. The more light the more you can see. When the light is dim, it is harder to see. How well can you see without any light?

WHAT DO I DO?

1. Sit on the floor. Ask your friend to tie the blindfold over your eyes. Make sure you cannot see anything.

2. Ask your friend to put the 'mystery' objects inside the tin or box and close the lid.

3. Double check that there is no light coming through the blindfold. Open the tin or box and take out the objects, one at a time. Can you see what they are? Try to find out what they are by feeling them. Tell your friend what you think each mystery object is.

1

4. Slowly lift the blindfold. How far do you have to lift it before you can see if you were right?

WHAT HAPPENED?
You cannot see what your objects are when you are blindfolded because the blindfold has blocked out the light. Seeing is one of our five senses. When there is no light, we use some of our other senses, such as touch or smell, to find out what things are.

REFLECTING LIGHT

30 mins

When light shines on certain materials some or all of the light can 'bounce' back. This is called reflected light.

WHAT DO I NEED?

- several different materials, including some that are rough and smooth, shiny and dull
- small mirror, something metal, something made of hard plastic
- torch
- large piece of card

WHAT DO I DO?

1. Make a collection of different materials. Predict which ones will reflect the light best.

2. Now do the test, preferably in a darkened room. Shine the torch at an angle onto the material being tested. Put the card in a position to catch any reflected light. If the material reflects light well, you will see the circular shape of the torch light on the white card. Test the mirror first.

3. Now test the other materials in the same way.

4. Which materials reflected the light well? Which reflected the light best? Were the results as you predicted?

5. Sort the materials into two groups – good and poor reflectors.

WHAT HAPPENED?

Smooth, shiny objects reflect more light than dull, rough objects. The mirror is designed to reflect most light. Almost all the light bounces off a mirror – that is why you can see yourself!

23

30 mins

BLOCKING LIGHT

Light passes through some things, but not through others. Before you begin the experiment, predict which of your test materials will let most light through and which will let least light through.

WHAT DO I NEED?

- scissors
- shoe box
- ruler
- small toy
- hand torch
- sticky tape
- book
- test materials (e.g. pieces of paper, cloth, clear plastic, cling film, aluminium foil, tissue paper)
- pencil and paper

WHAT DO I DO?

1. Ask an adult to cut a hole about 15cm x 10cm in the top of the shoe box lid, and a square of about 3cm in one side of the shoe box.

2. Put the toy inside the box and put the lid on.

1

 You will need an adult to help you make the box.

3. Position the end of the torch over the hole in the side and tape it securely to hold it in place. You may need to rest the torch on something, such as a book. Switch on the torch.

4. Lay your test materials, one at a time, over the hole in the lid, completely covering it. What can you see? Make a record of the results.

WHAT HAPPENED?

You can see the torchlight and toy clearly through some materials. This is because almost all the light passes through these materials, from inside and outside the box. These materials are transparent.

Some materials let some light through them and block (reflect) the rest. You can see the torchlight glowing inside the box, but you cannot see the toy very clearly. These materials are translucent.

The other materials block all of the light, both from outside and inside the box. You cannot see inside the box at all. These materials are opaque.

MAKING
SHADOWS

10 mins

When light hits an object a shadow forms behind it. Find out what different shadows you can make with various objects, including your hands.

WHAT DO I NEED?
- torch
- mug
- building blocks
- white wall or screen
- transparent plastic bottle

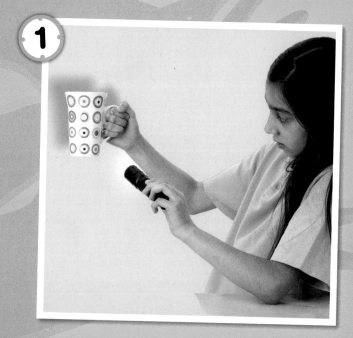

WHAT DO I DO?

1. Hold the mug about 4cm from the wall or screen, and shine the torch on it. What shape is the shadow?

2. Do you think that something that is transparent will create a shadow? Shine the torch onto the plastic bottle and see if you are right.

3. Make a stack of blocks. Shine the torch onto the stack. What happens to the shadow when you change the arrangement of the stack?

WHAT HAPPENED?
When light hits an object, some of the light is blocked but the rest travels on past the object. So the space behind the object is less well lit than the space around it. This forms a shadow that is exactly the same shape as the object.

MAKING
SHAPES

WHAT DO I NEED?

- torch
- your hands
- a friend

WHAT DO I DO?

Use your hands to make these shapes. Ask a friend to shine the torch on your hands to make the shadows. What shapes are the shadows? What other shapes can you make?

LIGHT TRAVELS IN STRAIGHT LINES

30 mins

Light does not bend around shapes like sound does. Light always travels in a straight line. This torch experiment proves it!

WHAT DO I NEED?

- torch
- 3 postcards
- sheet of A4 paper
- large nail
- modelling clay
- black card
- paper, pencil and ruler

1

WHAT DO I DO?

1. Hold the postcards so that the bottom edges are on top of each other. Make a hole through the middle using the nail.

2

2. Draw a pencil line down the centre of the paper. Lay three small lumps of clay along the pencil line about 3cm apart.

③

3. Place the black card in the furthest piece of clay. Place a postcard in each of the other two pieces so that the hole in the postcard is above the line on the paper.

④

4. Shine the torch through the hole in the first postcard. Tilt the torch slightly until the circle of light hits the hole in the second postcard. Can you see the light on the black card? Turn the torch a little to the left. What happens?

5. Add the third card in front of the other cards. Can you still get the beam to hit the black card?

6. Take away the postcard nearest the black card. Now take away the next postcard. What happens to the spot of light?

WHAT HAPPENED?

When the holes were lined up in a straight line, the beam travelled straight through them. The bigger the gap between the last hole and the black screen, the larger the final circle of light. This is because the light spreads out.

BOUNCING LIGHT

15 mins

Shiny objects reflect light because the light bounces off them. But can you predict which direction the reflected light will take? This experiment will work best in a dark or dim room.

WHAT DO I NEED?
- torch
- mirror

1

WHAT DO I DO?

1. Shine the torch into the mirror and look for the reflection of the light on the wall. Where do you think the reflected light will be if you angle the torch to the left?

2. Angle the torch to the left. Was your prediction correct? Now predict where the light will be when you angle the beam to the right, then up and then down. Test your predictions.

WHAT HAPPENED?

Light travels in straight lines, so, when it hit the mirror at an angle, it was reflected at an angle. Light is only reflected straight back to you when you point it straight at the mirror.

CAN LIGHT TURN A CORNER?

5 mins

Light travels only in straight lines, so is it possible to make it go round a corner? It is, if you reflect the light off a mirror!

WHAT DO I NEED?

- door
- hand mirror

WHAT DO I DO?

1. Stand just behind an open door.

2. Hold a hand mirror out in front of you and angle it until you can see what is on the other side of the door.

Door

You

Light from behind the door bounces off the mirror.

1

WHAT HAPPENED?

You can see what is on the other side of the door because the light from that side hits the mirror and bounces off it at an angle, into your eyes.

50 mins

EXPLORING SHADOWS

To make a shadow, you need a light, an object and a screen or surface to catch the shadow. This experiment explores how the length of the shadow changes as the distance between the object and the screen changes or the distance between the light and the object changes.

WHAT DO I NEED?

- torch
- object, such as a small plastic figure
- table
- white wall or screen
- ruler, paper and pencil

1

WHAT DO I DO?

1. Place the figure on the table 10cm from the screen. Place the torch on the table 30cm from the screen and shine it on the figure. Measure the height of the shadow and write it down.

2. Now move the figure so that it is 15cm from the screen.
Measure the height of the shadow again.
Repeat with the figure 20cm from the screen.

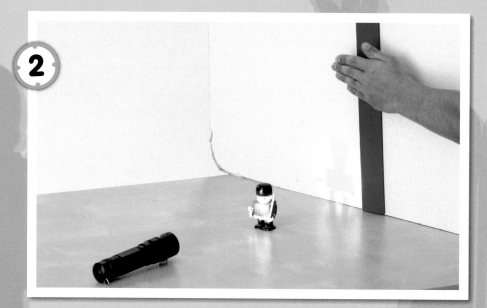

2

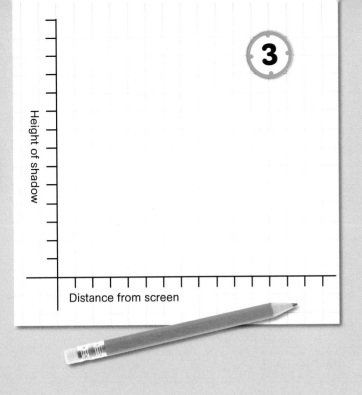

Height of shadow

Distance from screen

3. Make a graph to show how the size of the shadow changes as the figure is moved away from the screen.

4. Repeat the experiment, but this time keep the figure 10cm from the screen and move the torch towards it in 5cm jumps. What happens to the shadow?

5. Keep the figure on the table but change the height of the torch. Start with the torch 30cm behind the figure and 30cm above the table. Slowly lower the torch but keep it shining on the figure. What happens to the shadow?

WHAT HAPPENED?

The height of the shadow changes because light travels in straight lines. The top of the torch, the top of the object and the top of the shadow should all form a straight line. So the closer the object is to the screen, the smaller the shadow. The closer the light is to the figure, the larger the shadow.

As you lower the height of the torch you create a longer, less slanting line between the torch, the object and the shadow. The same thing happens as the Sun moves across the sky. Shadows are longest at dawn and dusk when the Sun is low in the sky and shortest when the Sun is highest in the sky.

IS IT MAGNETIC?

20 mins

Some objects stick to magnets, but others do not. Can you predict which of the test objects will be attracted to a magnet?

WHAT DO I NEED?

- pencil and a ruler
- sheet of paper
- strong magnet, such as a bar magnet
- test objects (e.g. a coin, an eraser, a key, a wooden spoon, a metal spoon, a plastic cup, some drawing pins, some scraps of paper)

1

2

WHAT DO I DO?

1. Use the pencil and ruler to divide your paper into three columns. Name the first column 'object', the second column 'guess', and the third column 'result'.

2. Write a list of your test objects in the first column.

4

3. In the second column, put a tick next to the objects you think will stick to the magnet, and a cross next to those you think will not.

4. Test each object in turn and put a tick or a cross in the third column. How many of your guesses were correct?

WHAT HAPPENED?

Objects that contain iron or steel stick to magnets. Iron and steel are magnetic materials. Other materials, such as tin, brass, paper and wood, are non-magnetic and do not stick to magnets.

MAGNETIC FORCE

25 mins

The pulling power of a magnet is a force called magnetism. This experiment compares how well two different magnets can pull a paperclip.

WHAT DO I NEED?
- pen and ruler
- piece of paper
- strong bar magnet
- some paperclips
- horseshoe magnet

WHAT DO I DO?

1. Use the ruler to make small dots 1cm apart along the long edge of the paper for 10cm. Now use the ruler to draw short lines as shown.

2. Draw a line across the page at the 10cm and 1cm marks, as shown below. These are your start and finish lines.

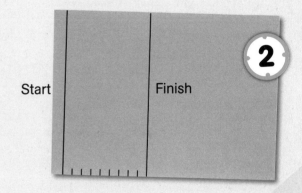

Start   Finish

3. Place the bar magnet on the finish line and the paperclip on the start line.

4. Slowly slide the bar magnet along the paper towards the paperclip. How far away is the magnet from the paperclip before anything happens?

5. Try the test again using the horseshoe magnet instead of the bar magnet. What happens?

WHAT HAPPENED?
Different magnets have different strengths. The farther away the magnet is when it attracts the paperclip, the stronger the magnet.

35

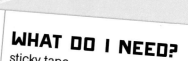

MAGNETIC POLES

The magnetic force of a magnet is stronger at the ends of the magnet than in the middle. The ends of the magnet are known as its poles. Sometimes the poles are marked with the letters 'N' and 'S', for north and south. This experiment explores what happens when two poles meet.

WHAT DO I NEED?

- sticky tape
- 2 toy cars
- 2 bar magnets, at least as long as the cars

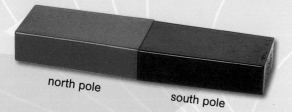

north pole   south pole

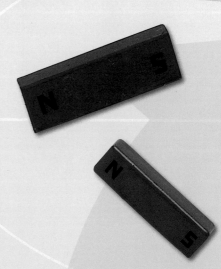

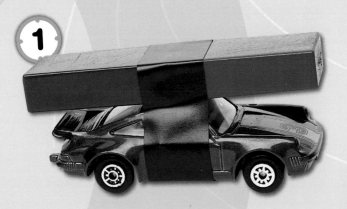

1

WHAT DO I DO?

1. Tape the middle of each magnet to the roof of a toy car. Make sure both magnets have the same pole pointing to the front of the car.

2. What happens when you push the front of one car towards the back of the other?

3. What happens when you push both cars face to face?

4. What happens if you put the cars back to back?

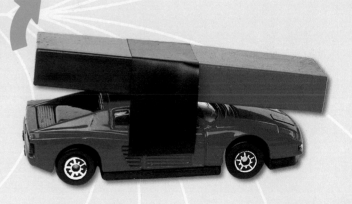

WHAT HAPPENED?

When one car is behind the other, the magnets pull the cars together. This is because the opposite poles are facing each other (north to south, or south to north). Opposite magnetic poles attract each other.

When the two cars are facing each other or when they are back to back, the magnets push the cars apart. This is because the same poles are facing each other (north to north or south to south). The same magnetic poles repel, or push away from each other.

15 mins

MAKE A MAGNET HOVER

This experiment uses the pushing power of magnets to make a magnet hover in the air.

WHAT DO I NEED?

- 3 doughnut magnets
- coloured paper
- scissors
- glue stick or sticky tape
- piece of dowelling rod almost as thick as the hole in the magnets
- modelling clay

WHAT DO I DO?

1. Find out which side of your magnets stick together. As opposite poles attract, one side will be a north pole, the other a south pole.

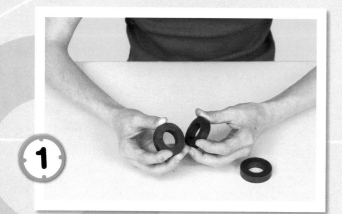

2. Cut out and glue or tape a small square of coloured paper onto the north side of each magnet.

3. Push the dowelling rod into a lump of modelling clay so that it stands upright.

4. Slide magnet 1 onto the dowelling rod north side up, magnet 2 north side down, and magnet 3 north side up. What happens to the magnets?

WHAT HAPPENED?

Magnets 2 and 3 hover because each has the same pole facing the magnet below it. It is impossible to make two poles that are the same touch! Without the dowelling rod the magnets would slip sideways and drop to the table, but the rod holds them in place, keeping the poles facing each other.

DO MAGNETS WORK THROUGH GLASS AND WATER?

10 mins

Glass and water are non-magnetic materials. Do non-magnetic materials block magnetism, or can the force of a magnet work through them? What is your prediction?

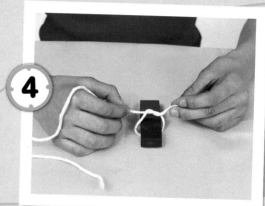

WHAT DO I DO?

1. Almost fill the glass jar with water.

2. Drop in the paperclip and let it sink to the bottom of the jar.

3. What happens if you hold the magnet to the outside of the jar near the paperclip? Can you make the paperclip move? Can you lift it to the top of the jar?

4. Repeat step 2, but this time tie a length of string around the magnet and lower it into the water. Will it pick up the paperclip?

WHAT HAPPENED?

If your magnet is strong enough, you can use it to slide the paperclip up the side of the glass jar because its magnetic force passes through the glass and the water to pull on the paperclip. If you put the magnet into the water it will still work on the paperclip – because water is non-magnetic and does not block the magnetic force.

39

WHAT MAKES SOUND?

15 mins

When something vibrates, it makes a sound. A vibration is a tiny, fast movement backwards and forwards. Sound makes something vibrate many times a second. In this experiment you can feel the vibrations as well as hear the sound.

WHAT DO I NEED?
- large round balloon
- a friend

WHAT DO I DO?

1. Blow up the balloon and tie it. Hold it by the knot.

2. Ask a friend to put his or her hand against one side of the balloon.

3. Put your mouth against the other side of the balloon. Say the letters of the alphabet slowly and clearly.

4. Find out which of the sounds your friend can feel most easily. Record your results in a table. What is the sound travelling through inside the balloon?

WHAT HAPPENED?
Saying the letters created vibrations, which made the balloon vibrate. The vibrations travelled through the air inside the balloon to the opposite side. The letters that involve moving your lips, such as B, M, P, W and Y, probably created the strongest vibrations.

40

20 mins

SEE THE VIBRATIONS!

Most vibrations are too fast to see, but this experiment lets you do just that.

WHAT DO I DO?

1. Cut a piece of plastic bag that is a few centimetres larger than the top of the biscuit tin.

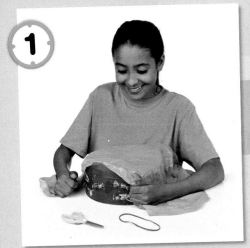

2. Cover the open top of the biscuit tin with the plastic and secure it in place with the elastic band.

3. Firmly but steadily pull the plastic tight in all directions across the top of the biscuit tin.

4. Place the sequins on the plastic. Bring the metal lid to about 10cm above them and strike the lid with the spoon.

5. What happens to the sequins when you bang the lid? Repeat the experiment using grains of rice, then salt, and then sugar. Which jumps the highest?

WHAT HAPPENED?

When the lid was hit, it vibrated. This caused the air around it to vibrate. The vibrations passed into the plastic cover of the tin, making the sequins jump up and down. Sugar and salt may jump the most because they are the lightest.

20 mins

HOW DO YOU HEAR SOUNDS?

Your two ears work together to gather sounds that reach them through the air. The outer ears collect the sound waves and funnel them into the ear canals. What would happen if one ear was blocked? Do this experiment to find out.

WHAT DO I NEED?

- 2 coins
- chair
- a friend
- piece of card about 40cm x 30cm
- large paperclip
- sticky tape
- scissors

WHAT DO I DO?

1. Sit on a chair and close your eyes. Ask a friend to move round you, about 2m away, and click the coins. After each click, point to where you think you heard them. Cover each ear in turn and repeat.

2. Fold the card to make a cone and secure it with a large paperclip. Use a strip of sticky tape to join the overlap.

3. Cut off the pointed bit of the cone so that it fits over your ear hole but does not go inside it.

4. Ask a friend to whisper to you from a distance of about 1m without using your ear trumpet and again with your ear trumpet in place.

WHAT HAPPENED?

Both ears are used to locate sound so, if one is damaged or covered up, it is more difficult to tell where a sound is coming from. The ear trumpet makes a whisper easier to hear.

WHAT DOES SOUND TRAVEL THROUGH?

10 mins

WHAT DO I NEED?

- 2 plastic cups
- sharp tool like a skewer or scissors
- string (about 3m)

Sound travels through air and this is how most of the sounds we hear reach our ears. But can sound travel through solid things too? Make a simple string telephone to find out.

WHAT DO I DO?

1. Ask an adult to help you make a small hole in the base of each cup with the sharp tool.

2. Thread one end of the string through one cup and tie a knot in it, on the inside of the cup. Thread the other end through the other cup and tie it in the same way.

3

3. Ask a friend to hold a cup, walk away from you until the string is tight, and speak quietly into it. While your friend is speaking, hold the other cup next to your ear. Can you hear what is being said through your 'telephone'?

4

4. Move closer to your friend and try the 'telephone' again when the string is not pulled tight. Does your telephone work as well?

WHAT HAPPENED?

Sound can move through solids (and liquids). When the string is pulled tight, sound vibrations pass easily along the string. The cups help to magnify and direct the sound into your ear. When the string is loose, the vibrations get lost.

30 mins

STOP THE NOISE!

Sometimes sounds are too loud. Very loud sounds can damage your ears, while other sounds can just be irritating. Materials that absorb sound well are called insulators. Test different materials to see how well they muffle sound.

WHAT DO I NEED?

- noise-maker, such as an alarm clock
- box (with a lid), big enough for the alarm clock and insulation
- cotton wool balls
- measuring tape
- pieces of newspaper screwed up into balls
- bubble wrap
- packing peas
- MP3 player or other sound-recording device

WHAT DO I DO?

1. Switch on the alarm clock so it's ringing and put it in the empty box. Close the lid.

2. Walk away from the box until you can no longer hear the sound. Measure how far you have walked.

3. Record the sound coming from the box at a distance of 1m.

4. Open the box and pack in the cotton wool balls around the clock, then close the lid again. Repeat steps 2 and 3. Test the other insulating materials in turn.

5. Listen to all the recordings to find out which material muffles the sound best.

WHAT HAPPENED?

When sound waves reach a material, some are absorbed and some are reflected away. Only some of the sound gets through. Material with a soft, rough surface will absorb the most sound.

20 mins

EXPLORING VOLUME

The more energy that goes into making a sound, the louder it is and the further it travels. Say a word, then shout it. Shouting uses more energy and so makes a louder sound. Now try shaking some noise!

WHAT DO I NEED?

- collection of containers with lids (e.g. yoghurt and cream pots, plastic bottles, card tubes)
- shaking materials (e.g. rice, paperclips, buttons, aquarium gravel)
- sticky tape
- MP3 player or other sound-recording device
- metre rule

WHAT DO I DO?

1. Take a container and fill it enough to cover the bottom with one of the shaking materials.

2. Close the container and seal it tightly. Rattle it first with slow, small shakes then increase the speed and size of the shakes.

3. Set up your sound recording device 1m away and make as large a sound as you can with the shaker.

4. Try different combinations of container and shaking material. Repeat steps 1–3.

5. Listen to all the recordings to find which combination makes the largest sound.

WHAT HAPPENED?

The contents that make the loudest sounds are those which are large with hard surfaces and are free to move. They make the loudest sound of all when they are shaken in the container with the hardest surface.

30 mins

MAKING PAN-PIPES

Pan-pipes are a musical instrument which comes from South America. The pitch of a note is how high or low it is. Find out how to make different notes by making your own set of pan-pipes.

WHAT DO I NEED?
- length of narrow plastic piping (about 1m long)
- hacksaw to cut the pipe
- coloured sticky tape
- stickers, ribbon (for decoration)

WHAT DO I DO?

1. Ask an adult to cut the pipe with the hacksaw into a range of lengths from long to short.

2. Arrange the pieces of pipe next to each other, in order of length. Tape them together and then decorate them.

46

3. First practice getting different notes from your pipes by blowing over the top of the pipes. You may need to practise to get a good note. Then blow over the top of the longest pipe. What sound does it make?

4. Now blow over the next pipe that is a little bit shorter. What do you notice about the sound? Is the note higher or lower?

5. What kind of note do you think the next pipe will make? Try it and see if you were right. Try blowing over all the other pipes. What do you notice about the notes?

6. Use your pan-pipes to make up your own tunes.

WHAT HAPPENED?

The shorter the tube the higher the pitch so the higher the note. The longest tube gives the lowest note. The same is true for other instruments. For example, using your finger to shorten a guitar string, gives a higher note.

15 mins

WHAT ARE SOLIDS?

Warning! Be careful using sharp tools – do not cut yourself.

Liquids and gases change shape easily. In fact they take the shape of the container they are in. Solids, however, change their shape only when something else forces them to change.

WHAT DO I NEED?

- some solid objects (e.g. a piece of cloth, modelling clay, coins, cheese, a ball, a plastic ruler, wooden sticks, paper, margarine, grapes, peas)
- tools (e.g. scissors, a plastic knife, a large stone)
- pencil and paper

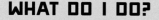

WHAT DO I DO?

1. Test your solids to find out how many ways you can change their shape. Try folding, squashing, stretching, bending, cutting, squeezing and breaking them.

2. Make a list of your solids and the ways in which each one can be changed.

1

WHAT HAPPENED?

The shape of some solids is easy to change because the solids are soft or bendy. Other solids are difficult to change because the material is very hard – it cannot easily be cut or broken.

3. Which solids are difficult to change and which are easy? Why do you think this is?

48

15 mins

COMPARING SOLIDS AND LIQUIDS

You can pour a liquid. For example, you can pour milk from a container to a glass. The milk takes the shape of the glass. Can a solid ever behave like a liquid?

WHAT DO I NEED?

- glass of water
- large bowl
- jar of syrup
- spoon
- saucers containing solids of different sizes (e.g. tomatoes, flour, pebbles, peas)

WHAT DO I DO?

1. Tip the glass of water into the bowl. What happens?

2. Clean and dry the bowl. Tip a spoonful of syrup into it. How is it different from the water? Clean the bowl.

4. How do the solids compare with the water and syrup?

3. Tip each saucer of solids into the bowl in turn, cleaning the bowl each time.

WHAT HAPPENED?

The tomatoes do not pour because each tomato is a single lump of material. The pebbles, peas and flour look as if they are pouring but only because each small piece is falling at the same time as the other pieces around it. None of the pieces change shape when they hit the bowl. When liquids are poured, even thick liquids such as syrup, they spread out to form a level surface within the container.

15 mins

ICE AND WATER

When water gets very cold it freezes. That is it changes from a liquid to become solid ice. Water freezes at 0° Celsius. Find out what else happens when water turns to ice.

WHAT DO I NEED?
- balloon
- water
- sink
- pen
- tape measure
- freezer
- large bowl

WHAT DO I DO?

1. Carefully put the opening of your balloon over a tap. Turn the tap on and slowly fill the balloon about 3/4 full with water. Tie it up.

2. Draw a line around the widest part of the balloon. Measure this distance with the tape measure and record the result.

50

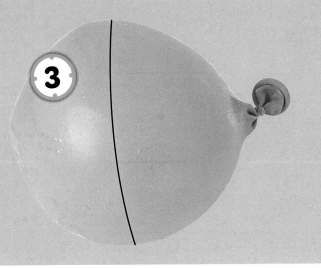

3. Put the balloon in a freezer for a few hours or overnight.

4. Take it out and look closely to see what has happened.

5. Measure the balloon again along the line you made with the pen.

6. Has the balloon got bigger or smaller? What do you think has happened to the water inside the balloon as it changed from a liquid to a solid? Has it changed in other ways?

7. Try floating your ice balloon in a large bowl of water.

WHAT HAPPENED?

When you put the balloon in the freezer, the water inside it changed to ice. When you measured the line around the middle of the frozen balloon, you should have found that it was longer. In other words, the frozen balloon is bigger than the balloon filled with water. This is because ice takes up more space than the same amount of water.

The frozen balloon floats because it is now less dense than water. This means it is lighter for its size.

MELTING SOLIDS

15 mins

When a solid melts, it turns into a liquid. This experiment compares what it takes to melt different solids.

WHAT DO I NEED?
- pencil and a ruler
- piece of paper
- some test solids (e.g. an ice cube, a square of butter, a piece of chocolate, a candle)
- 4 saucers

1

WHAT DO I DO?

1. Put the ice cube, butter, chocolate and candle onto separate saucers.

2. Leave the saucers in a warm place, such as a sunny windowsill.

3. Check the saucers every 10 minutes for the next 30–40 minutes. Every time you check the saucers, record on a chart how the solids look.

WHAT HAPPENED?

The ice cube melts quickly because it has a low melting point – the temperature at which a solid turns into a liquid. Butter and chocolate have higher melting points so they take longer to melt. The candle does not melt because it is not hot enough. Ask an adult to light the candle and watch what happens.

15 mins

CHANGING SHAPE BY HEATING AND COOLING

Solids melt to become liquid when they are heated. They solidify, or become solid, when they cool down. Can you change the shape of solid chocolate by heating and cooling it?

WHAT DO I NEED?

- greaseproof baking paper
- baking tray
- pastry cutters
- half a bar of chocolate
- glass jug or double boiler
- coloured sweets
- helpful adult

WHAT DO I DO?

1. Cover the baking tray with greaseproof paper. Put the pastry cutters on the tray with the patterned edge face down.

2. Break the chocolate into squares. Ask an adult to melt the squares in a microwave oven or in a bowl over water in a pan on the stove until the chocolate is runny.

4. Put the baking tray in the fridge until the chocolate has nearly set. Then decorate the chocolate shapes with sweets and put the baking tray back in the fridge.

3. Pour the chocolate into the pastry cutters so that it is about half a centimetre deep.

5. When the chocolate has set, gently push the shapes out of the cutters. What shape is the chocolate now?

WHAT HAPPENED?

Liquid chocolate can be poured into a mould. When the liquid cools, the chocolate becomes solid again. But the chocolate squares do not go back to their old shape. Instead they take the shape of the mould.

25 mins

VANISHING WATER

Where does water go when a puddle dries up? Where does rain come from? Could it be the same water? Find the answers by doing these two experiments on the water cycle.

WHAT DO I NEED?
- transparent bowl
- modelling clay
- toy model village
- jug of hot water from the tap
- plastic film

WHAT DO I DO?

1. Make the banks of a lake with the modelling clay, about a third of the way up the sides of the transparent bowl. Add small toy models of animals, trees and houses to create a scene.

2. Fill the lake with hot water. Ask an adult to help.

3. Quickly stretch the plastic film over the top of the bowl and seal it along the edge by pressing it firmly.

4. Watch as water droplets appear on the inside of the bowl and the film. Where does this water come from? Can you see the droplets of water on the film fall like rain and run down the sides of the bowl?

WHAT HAPPENED?

Some of the hot water evaporated, which means it changed into water gas. As the water gas cooled, it condensed and so changed back into droplets of water. The same thing happens on a much larger scale on the surface of Earth. Water evaporates from oceans, lakes and so on. Water gas rises into the air, where it cools to form clouds. Water from clouds eventually falls back to Earth's surface as rain.

PLOTTING A PUDDLE

45 mins

WHAT DO I NEED?

- jug of water
- chalk
- pen and paper
- clock

WHAT DO I DO?

1. On a sunny day, make a puddle by pouring water onto some hard ground. Draw around the puddle with chalk.

2. Return to the puddle regularly and draw around it each time. How does the shape of the puddle change? Draw the shape on the paper each time.

WHAT HAPPENED?

The water in the puddle evaporated into the air. The hotter the sunshine, the quicker water evaporates. As the puddle dries up, there is less water to evaporate, so a puddle can evaporate faster as it becomes shallower.

15 mins

WHAT DOES ELECTRICITY DO?

Electricity is a type of energy, which makes all sorts of things work. How many things in your home are powered by electricity?

WHAT DO I NEED?
- paper
- pen

WHAT DO I DO?

1. Draw a straight line down the middle of the piece of paper.

2. In the left-hand column, list all the things in your house that use electricity.

3. In the right-hand column, write down what each machine does. Ask an adult if you are not sure.

4. Group the machines on your list according to what they do. For example, do they give out light or heat, or sounds and pictures, or make something move?

2

Lamp
Radio
TV

WHAT HAPPENS?

Electricity comes into the home through wires. The wires run inside the walls. We access electricity by plugging a machine into a wall socket. Electricity is used to run most machines in the home. The energy is changed into heat, or light or sound, or it makes part of the machine move.

10 mins

GETTING TO GRIPS WITH
BATTERIES

Batteries provide a small amount of electricity. This makes a battery safe to use. Batteries are easy to carry around and fit into small machines and devices, such as a torch. Find out how to place the batteries so that the torch works.

WHAT DO I NEED?

- torch that works

WHAT DO I DO?

1. Find out how to turn the torch on and off. Take out the batteries and examine them. Each one has a plus and a minus sign.

2. Put the batteries back in the torch and turn it on. Try turning each battery first one way round and then the other. Make a note of the positions of the plus and minus ends each time. How many ways can you get the torch to work?

WHAT HAPPENED?

The bulb lights up when the plus end of one battery is touching the minus end of the other battery. When both plus ends or both minus ends are together, the electricity cannot flow and the torch does not work.

⚠️ Batteries work using the chemicals they hold inside them. Batteries are safe to touch but DO NOT try to look inside one. The chemicals can burn you if they get onto your skin or clothes.

MAKING A SIMPLE CIRCUIT

10 mins

For electricity to work, it has to flow in a loop called a circuit. The electricity flows round and round the circuit. Find out how to connect different things to make a circuit.

WHAT DO I NEED?

- helpful adult
- scissors
- 2 lengths of single-strand, plastic-coated wire
- small screwdriver
- bulb holder
- small torch bulb of 3 volts (3V)
- AC or AA size battery (1.5V)
- sticky tape

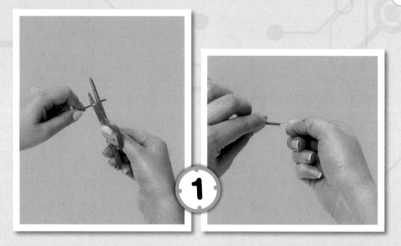

WHAT DO I DO?

1. Ask an adult to strip about 2cm of the coating off both ends of the wires. Twist the ends of the wires to make them neat.

2. Use the screwdriver to loosen the two screws on either side of the bulb holder. Twist one bared end of each wire around the base of the screws. Tighten the screws again to hold the wires in place.

3. Carefully screw the bulb into the bulb holder.

4. Tape the other ends of the wires to the positive and negative terminals of the battery. Make sure the bare wires are on the metal contact points of the battery. What happens to the light bulb?

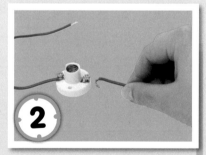

WHAT HAPPENED?

The bulb lights up because electricity is flowing from the battery along the wire, through the bulb and back to the battery again in an unbroken circuit.

15 mins

WILL IT WORK?

If any part of a circuit is connected up wrongly, the circuit will not work. Which of these circuits do you think will work and which won't? Experiment to find out.

WHAT DO I NEED?

- the same circuit parts you used to make a simple circuit (pages 58)
- A pencil and paper

WHAT DO I DO?

1. Look carefully at the following three circuits.

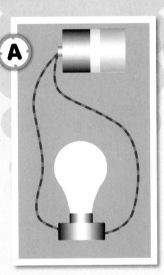

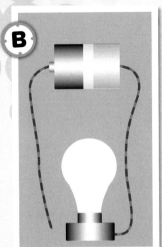

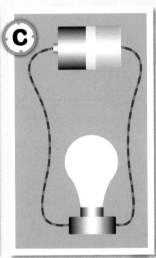

2. Write down which circuits you think will work and which will not.
Using the parts from the circuit you made on page 58, make each of the circuits A, B and C in turn. Were you right or wrong?

WHAT HAPPENED?

Circuit A does not work because both wires are connected to the same terminal on the battery. Circuit B does not work because the circuit is not complete. There is a break in the circuit between the bulb and the wire. Electricity must flow from one end of the battery to the other. Circuit C works because electricity can flow from the battery to the bulb, and back to the other end of the battery – the circuit is complete.

59

15 mins

MAKING A SWITCH

A switch is a device for turning a circuit on and off. Every electrical machine has a switch. Lights have switches too and a wall socket has a switch to turn it on and off. This experiment shows how a switch works.

WHAT DO I DO?

1. Connect up your circuit below and make sure the bulb lights up.

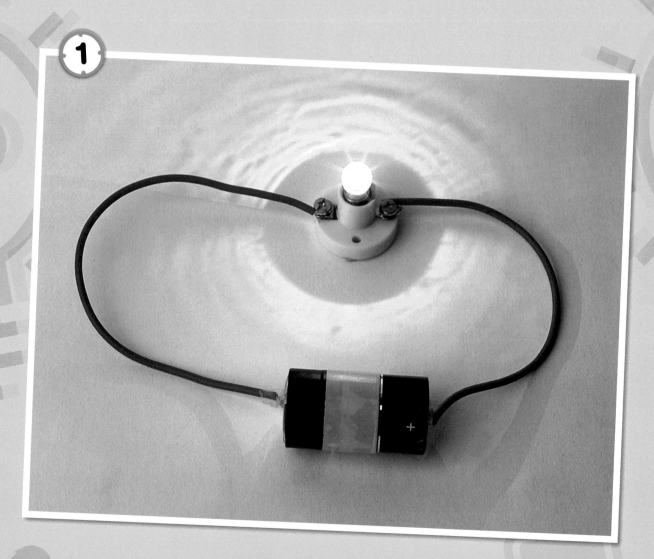

1

2. Take one of the wires off the bulb and wrap it securely around a drawing pin.

3. Push the drawing pin through a paperclip and into the balsa wood.

4. Connect the third piece of wire from the free end of the bulb to the other drawing pin.

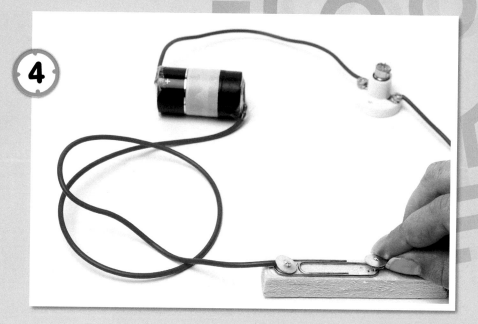

5. What happens when the paperclip touches just one of the drawing pins? What happens when the paperclip touches both drawing pins?

6. Can you find a way to arrange the paperclip so that it is easy to open and close the circuit?

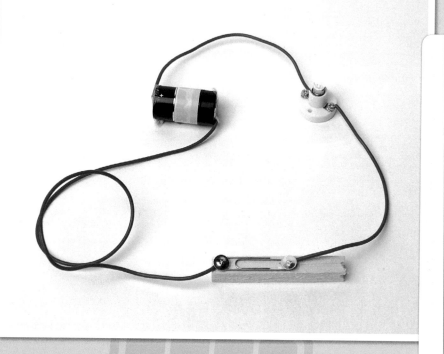

WHAT HAPPENED?

When the paperclip touches just one drawing pin the light is off because there is a gap in the circuit. Electricity cannot flow if there is a gap in a circuit. When the paperclip touches both drawing pins, the gap is closed and electricity flows around the circuit. The paperclip acts as a switch. Switches open or close a gap in a circuit.

WHICH MATERIALS ARE GOOD CONDUCTORS?

20 mins

Electricity flows through some materials more easily than others. Materials that carry electricity well are called conductors. Those that do not are called insulators. Test the materials in this experiment to see which are conductors and which are insulators.

WHAT DO I NEED?

- the same circuit parts you used to make a simple circuit on page 58
- extra length of single-strand plastic-coated wire
- some test materials (e.g. some wood, a plastic ruler, paper, aluminium foil, a glass, a metal paperclip, an eraser)
- pencil and paper

WHAT DO I DO?

1. Set up a simple circuit, but use the extra piece of wire to leave a gap in the circuit.

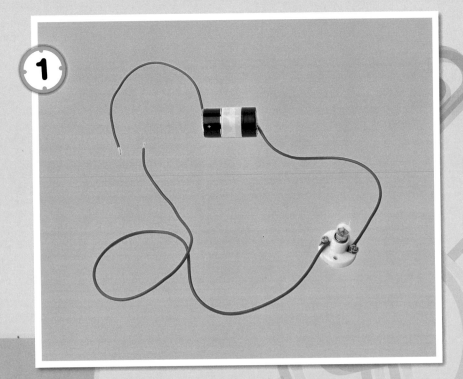

1

2. Touch the two ends of wire together to make sure your circuit is working properly.

3. Now touch the two ends to each of your test materials in turn.

4. Note down each material you use and whether or not the bulb lights up.

eraser
glass
no

WHAT HAPPENED?

The bulb lights up with metal objects because metal is a good conductor. It does not light up when the circuit includes materials such as plastic and wood – these materials are good insulators. Why do you think electric wires are coated in plastic?

MAKING A LIGHT BRIGHTER

20 mins

A circuit can have many parts, or components, attached to it. What happens when you add extra lights or extra batteries?

WHAT DO I DO?

1. Build a circuit using two lengths of wire, a 1.5V battery and one bulb.

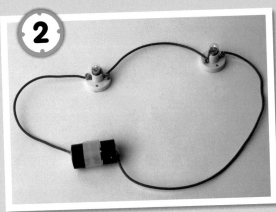

2. Add another length of wire and another bulb to your circuit. What happens? Do both bulbs glow?

3. Add a fourth length of wire and a third bulb. What happens now? Are all the bulbs lit? Are they brighter or dimmer?

4. Replace the 1.5V battery with the 9V battery. Does this make a difference?

WHAT HAPPENED?

When you add more bulbs to a low-voltage battery, the lights become dimmer. That's because each bulb gets a smaller share of the electricity. When you use a stronger battery, there is enough electricity for the bulbs to share between them and make them bright. But, if the battery is too powerful, the bulbs will burn out and stop working.

MAKE A MOTORISED AEROPLANE

30 mins

You can use electricity to run a motor and spin something round and round, as well as to light a lamp.

WHAT DO I NEED?

- thick card
- small motor
- paints
- strong glue
- tape
- wooden skewer
- paper fastener switch
- 1.5V battery in holder
- 3 pieces of wire with ends stripped
- plastic propeller (that fits exactly onto motor shaft)

WHAT DO I DO?

1. Make a circuit using the battery in its holder, wires, switch and motor as shown in the picture.

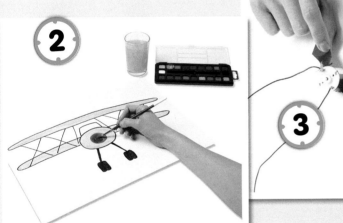

2. Paint a picture of the front of an aeroplane on the piece of thick card. Make a hole with the skewer where you want the centre of the propeller.

3. Push the motor shaft through this hole and tape the motor to the back of the picture.

4. Use strong glue to fix the propeller securely to the motor shaft.

5. Close the switch. What happens to the propeller?

WHAT HAPPENED?

Electricity in the circuit caused the motor to spin. The propeller spins because it is attached to the motor.

45 mins

CIRCUIT SYMBOL GAME

Do your friends know the correct symbols for the different electric components? Use electric circuits to make a quiz game to test them. The yellow box shows you the correct symbols to use.

WHAT DO I DO?

1. First make holes for the paper fasteners in the piece of card using the wooden skewer. You need two rows of four holes opposite each other as shown. Attach the fasteners.

WHAT DO I NEED?

- sheet of thick A4 card
- wooden skewer
- 8 paper fasteners
- 4 self-adhesive stickers
- marker pen
- 1.5V battery in a holder
- thin insulated wire with the ends stripped
- strong glue
- 1.5V battery
- motor
- 2 torch bulbs
- bulb holder
- switch
- A friend

2. Use strong glue to stick the motor, bulb, switch and battery onto the card next to the fasteners on the left as shown in the picture.

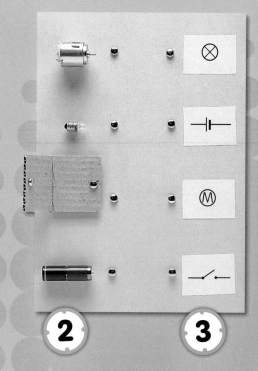

66

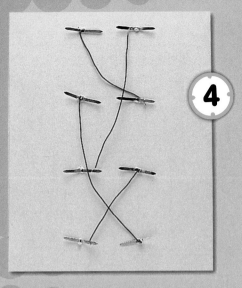

Name of component	Symbol
Battery	⊣⊢
Wire	—
Bulb	⊗ or ◷
Open switch	─╱ ─
Closed switch	─╱─
Motor	Ⓜ

3. Draw the symbol for a motor, a bulb, a switch and a battery on separate stickers. Stick each one onto the right-hand side of the board – but do NOT put the correct symbol next to the part it represents.

4. Turn the board over and wind short lengths of wire around the back of the fasteners, connecting each electric part to its correct symbol.

5. Make a broken circuit with a bulb like the one on page 62, which you used to test conductors. Your quiz game is now ready!

6. Ask a friend to match one of the parts to its symbol by placing one wire from the tester on the paper fastener next to the electric part and the other wire on the fastener next to the symbol he thinks is correct. How will you know if he is right? If he is wrong, he can try again – or let another friend have a go.

7. Design another matching quiz game which uses the same tester as this experiment, for example, match flags to their countries.

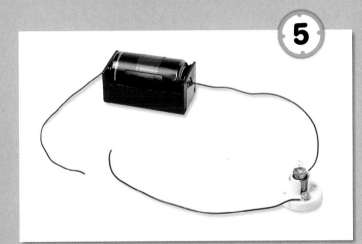

WHAT HAPPENED?
The wires at the back of your board connect the component to the correct symbol. When your friend makes the correct connection on the front of the board, the circuit is completed and the bulb lights up.

15 mins

IS IT SEE-THROUGH?

Some materials are transparent – we can see right through them. Some are opaque – this means we cannot see through them at all. Other materials are translucent – things look blurry through them. Predict which materials in this experiment will be transparent, opaque or translucent and then test to find out.

1. Hold the cardboard tube up to one eye, like a telescope, and check that you can see clearly through it.

2. Wrap each test material in turn over one end of the tube. Hold the test material in place with sticky tape or elastic bands. Look through the tube to discover if you can see through the material.

3. Which test materials can you see through? Is what you see clear or fuzzy?

4. Make a list of which test materials are transparent, which are translucent and which are opaque.

WHAT HAPPENED?
Were your predictions correct? Cling film is transparent and so are some plastic bags and sweet wrappers. Metal foil and felt are opaque. Tracing paper is translucent and cotton cloth may be too.

20 mins

TESTING FOR HARDNESS

Diamonds are the hardest material in the world. Scientists do a hardness test to compare materials. If you can scratch one material with another, the one that does the scratching is harder than the other.

WHAT DO I NEED?

- large nail
- plastic knife or fork,
- wooden cocktail stick
- sharp stone
- surfaces to test, such as: an old saucepan, the plastic lid from a yoghurt pot, a stone, a piece of wood
- paper and pen

WHAT DO I DO?

1. Try scratching the saucepan with the plastic knife, the cocktail stick, the stone and the nail. Will any of them make a scratch? If they do, they are harder than the pan. Make a note of the results.

2. Try scratching the wood with the nail, the plastic knife and the stone. Are all the scratchers harder than the wood? Do the same with the plastic lid.

3. Try scratching the stone with the nail, the wooden cocktail stick and the plastic knife. Are any of the scratchers harder than the stone?

4. Analyse your results. Can you make a scale of hardness?

WHAT HAPPENED?

The nail and the stone are probably the best scratchers. Did the nail scratch the stone? If so, it is the hardest. It is unlikely that the plastic fork or the cocktail stick scratched anything, but did you manage to scratch the plastic lid?

69

30 mins

WHICH SOLIDS DISSOLVE?

Some solids mix so well with liquids that it looks as if the solid has disappeared. When this happens, we say that the solid has dissolved.

WHAT DO I NEED?
- pencil and ruler
- piece of paper
- jug of water
- some empty glass tumblers
- some test materials (e.g. salt, peas, pasta shapes, soil, powder paint, sugar, instant coffee, sand, flour)
- teaspoon
- mug
- liquids (e.g. milk, cool tea or coffee, orange juice)

WHAT DO I DO?

1. Use the pencil and ruler to divide your paper into three columns. Head them: 'material', 'guess' and 'result'.

2. Make a list of your test materials in the first column. In the second column, tick the test materials that you think will dissolve.

3. Half fill each glass with water. Stir a spoonful of a different test material into each one.

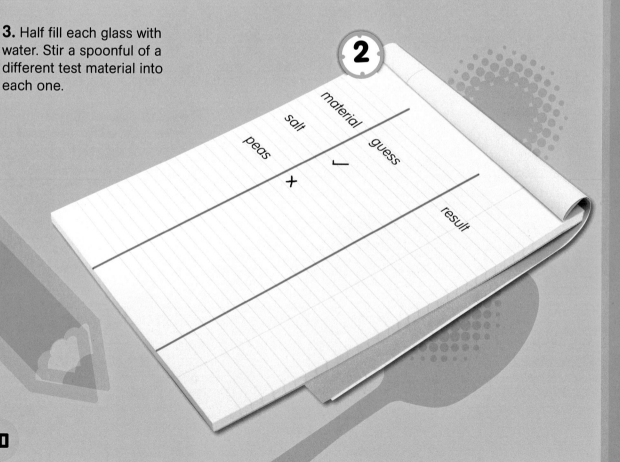

4. What happens to the solid in each glass? In the results column, tick the test materials that did dissolve. How many did you get right?

5. Repeat the test using the solid materials with different liquids in a mug, such as cool tea, coffee and orange juice. Are the results the same or different?

WHAT HAPPENED?

When a solid dissolves in water, it breaks up into such tiny pieces that you can no longer see them. They are said to be soluble. Some of the other solids make the water look cloudy. They are so light they float in the liquid for a while, but they have not dissolved. Eventually they sink to the bottom of the glass. All materials that sink to the bottom of the glass are insoluble. Milk, tea, coffee and orange juice are mostly water, so you should have got the same results as with plain water.

10 mins

SEPARATING A DISSOLVED SOLID

When a solid dissolves in a liquid, it seems to disappear. Is it possible to get it back again? This experiment does just that.

WHAT DO I DO?

1. Pour the warm water into the saucer.

2. Add the salt to the water and stir it until the salt dissolves.

3. Leave the saucer near a radiator or somewhere sunny for about four hours. Look at it again. What has happened?

2

WHAT HAPPENED?

The water in the saucer slowly disappears and only small solid bits of salt are left. This is because the water has evaporated – the heat from the radiator or Sun has turned the water into a gas and it has risen into the air. Dissolved solids can be separated from liquids by evaporation.

20 mins

MAKING CRYSTALS

A crystal is a solid particle with a symmetrical shape. Different solids form different shapes of crystals. This experiment uses Epsom salts because they form crystals within two hours. You can buy Epsom salts from a pharmacy.

WHAT DO I NEED?

- Epsom salts (you must wash hands thoroughly after handling Epsom salts)
- black plastic tray
- magnifying glass
- tablespoon
- clear plastic cup
- clear plastic tray
- paintbrush
- warm water.

WHAT DO I DO?

1. Put four tablespoonfuls of warm water into the plastic cup on the black tray. Add a teaspoon of Epsom salts and stir it in. Look in the bottom to see if they have all dissolved. Keep adding and stirring until some crystals are left undissolved at the bottom of the cup.

2. Dip the paintbrush in the Epsom salts solution and paint the bottom of one clear tray. Leave it in a warm dry place and check it every half an hour for signs of crystals.

3. When the solution has dried (the water has evaporated), use your magnifying glass to look for crystals. You could hold up the tray to a light (but not the Sun) to see them more clearly.

WHAT HAPPENED?

Crystals form when a solution is evaporated to reveal the dissolved solids. In step 1 you added as much Epsom salts as the water could hold. This made a strong solution that quickly evaporated to grow crystals.

SEPARATING A MIXTURE
OF SOLIDS

10 mins

A mixture of solids contains several different types of solid cut into small pieces and mixed together. This experiment shows you a quick and scientific way to separate the ingredients of a mixture.

WHAT DO I NEED?
- 2 large bowls
- cupful each of dried pasta, dried beans, oats, raisins, sugar, flour
- colander
- flour sieve

WHAT DO I DO?

1. Put all the solids in a bowl and mix them together. How does the mixture look? Can you see the separate pieces?

2. Pour the mixture through the colander into the other bowl. What happens?

3. Take away the colander and whatever is in it and pour the second bowl through the sieve into the empty bowl. What happens?

4. Which solids are left in the colander? Which solids are left in the sieve, and which are left in the final bowl?

WHAT HAPPENED?

When you pour the mixture through the colander some of the solids are left behind. This is because they are too big to pass through the holes. When you pour the remaining mixture through the sieve, only the flour and sugar are small enough to pass through the sieve holes. If you had a very fine sieve you could separate the sugar from the flour, too.

CHANGING A SOLID

20 mins

Some natural materials can be changed into other types of materials. These materials would not exist if people did not make them. This experiment requires the help of a responsible adult. With their help, you will see plaster of Paris powder change into hard plaster.

WHAT DO I NEED?
- a responsible adult to prepare and pour the plaster of Paris
- block of modelling clay
- rolling pin
- strip of card about 5cm wide and 50cm long
- plaster of Paris powder
- clean jug
- Water

WHAT DO I DO?

1. Roll out the clay into a round, flat base, at least 1cm thick and a little bigger than your hand.

2. Press your flat hand firmly into the clay. Lift up your hand so that you leave its shape printed in the clay.

3. Curve the strip of card into a circle that fits around your handprint. Press it gently into the clay so that it stays in place.

4. IMPORTANT Ask an adult to put some plaster of Paris in the jug and mix it with water until it forms a creamy paste.

5. Ask an adult to pour the paste into the card circle so that it completely covers the handprint. Leave the paste to dry. Do not touch it.

6. When the paste is completely dry, peel away the clay and the card. You are left with a hard plaster model of your hand.

WHAT HAPPENED?
The plaster of Paris changed from a soft powder into a hard plaster because it was mixed with water and left in the open air. Many materials are changed by mixing them with other materials. Sometimes they change when they are heated.

MAKE A VOLCANO

5 mins

When some stuff is mixed together a violent reaction can take place. This happens because the stuff in the mixture forms new substances quickly, and one of these new substances is a gas. The gas bubbles up in the mixture and makes it spill out of its container. We can make a cola fountain just by using diet cola and Mentos. Watch out – they react violently together!

WHAT DO I NEED?

- 500ml bottle of diet cola
- packet of Mentos (or other softmint sweets)
- narrow tube
- strip of card
- flat dish

WHAT DO I DO?

1. Open the bottle of diet cola and place it in a flat dish.

2. Place the strip of card over one end of the tube and lower it onto the bottle. Slide five or six Mentos into the top of the tube.

3. Pull the strip of paper away so that the sweets fall into the bottle and move the tube away quickly. Sit well back!

WHAT HAPPENED?

The eruption will start very quickly and may last for several seconds. The height of the cola fountain will depend on how many Mentos are used. The reaction will be more violent if a larger bottle of diet cola is used – and it is recommended that this is done outside. When volcanic lava turns into a solid, it does what every liquid does – it freezes. The rock freezes because its temperature goes below its freezing point.

MAKING PLASTIC FROM MILK

15 mins

Most types of plastic are made from oil, but not all. This experiment shows you how to make a plastic called casein from milk.

WHAT DO I NEED?

- warm water
- bowl
- plastic cup
- milk
- vinegar
- sieve
- tablespoon
- plate

WHAT DO I DO?

1. Pour warm water into the bowl and half fill the cup with milk. Put the cup in the bowl of water to warm up.

2. Add a tablespoon of vinegar to the warm milk and stir. Leave for five minutes and stir again.

3. Pour the milk and vinegar mixture into a sieve and let the water collect in the bowl below.

4. Scrape out the white solid from the sieve and place it on a plate. Make it into a disc and leave for a few days.

WHAT HAPPENED?

When you add the vinegar, the milk curdles and forms lumps of casein. The lumps stick together and form a larger lump, which becomes harder and more yellow. The warmer the water, the faster the casein forms.

THE SUN AND PLANETS

1 hour

The planets move around the Sun in oval-shaped paths, called orbits. This model shows how the planets orbit the Sun. It uses circular orbits instead of elliptical (oval-shaped) ones.

WHAT DO I NEED?
- large pieces of thin card
- ruler
- pair of compasses
- pencil
- scissors
- paper fastener
- sticky tape
- stopwatch or other timer

WHAT DO I DO?

1. Use the ruler and compasses to make nine card circles with diameters of 22cm, 20cm, 18cm, 16cm, 14cm, 12cm, 10cm, 8cm and 5cm.

2. Cut out the circles and make a small hole in the centre of each. Pile up the circles starting with the largest at the bottom. Link them with the paper fastener through the middle.

3. Cut eight card strips, 1cm wide by 4cm long. Bend them in the middle and attach one to the edge of each circle with sticky tape.

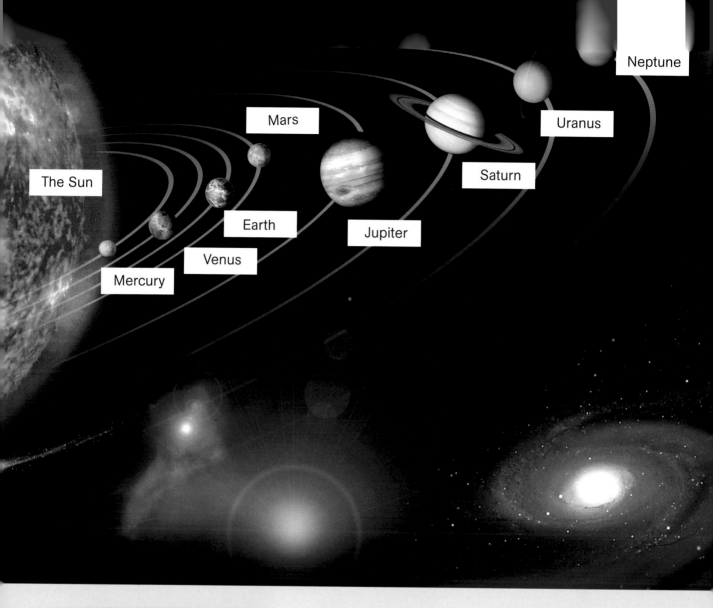

Neptune

Mars

Uranus

The Sun

Saturn

Earth

Jupiter

Venus

Mercury

4 **4.** Draw each of the planets on a piece of card, using the illustration above as a guide. Cut them out and attach them to the card strips in order, with Mercury on the smallest ring and Neptune on the largest.

5. Think of the paper fastener as the Sun. Gently move each planet round it in an anti-clockwise direction. Time how long it takes you to move each planet one full circle. Make a table to record and compare your results.

WHAT HAPPENED?

A year is the time it takes a planet to do a full circuit of the Sun. Mercury is the planet closest to the Sun and so it makes one orbit in the smallest amount of time. Neptune is the farthest planet and so it should take the longest.

CHANGING SHAPE OF THE MOON

On a clear night you can usually see the Moon, but the shape of the Moon changes over the course of a month. This experiment will help you to understand why.

WHAT DO I NEED?

- 2 large sheets of thin card
- pair of compasses
- pencil
- ruler
- scissors
- paper fastener
- metallic pen or white pencil
- ball of modelling clay (2–3cm in diameter)
- torch
- spare lump of modelling clay

WHAT DO I DO?

1. Cut a circle 14cm in diameter from one sheet of card. Cut a square 16cm x 16cm from the other sheet. Lay the circle over the square and push the paper fastener through the middle.

2. Press the ball of modelling clay onto the edge of the circle. This is the Moon. Mark an E (for Earth) on the opposite edge of the circle. Place the model along the edge of a table.

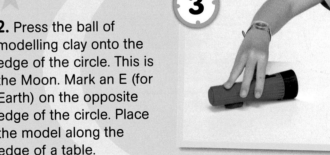

3. Shine the torch (the Sun) at an angle of 45° to the model from about 16cm away. Use the spare modelling clay to make the light shine horizontally.

4. Turn the circle of card so that the Moon is nearest to the torch. Look at the Moon from the point marked E. Draw the shape you see. Turn the circle 90° anti-clockwise and draw the shape you see from E. Repeat twice more.

WHAT HAPPENED?

As the Moon moves round the Earth, we see different amounts of its surface lit by the Sun. The lit-up areas are called phases of the Moon.

SUN'S CHANGING SHADOWS

45 mins

As the Earth rotates during the daytime, the Sun appears to move across the sky. You can trace the path of the Sun by watching where it casts shadows. Never look directly at the Sun – it can seriously damage your eyes.

WHAT DO I NEED?

- wooden or plastic board
- white paper
- sticky tape
- ruler
- 2 pencils
- compass
- piece of modelling clay
- clock

WHAT DO I DO?

1. Stick the white paper to the board with sticky tape. Mark halfway down one long side and draw a line straight across the paper to the other side.

2. Stand a pencil in the modelling clay at one end of the line across the paper.

3. Find an open space where there are no shadows from buildings or trees. Find north on the compass and set the board with the pencil side to the south (or north if you are in the southern hemisphere).

4. At 8 am on a sunny day, mark the length of the pencil's shadow on the paper. Repeat every hour until 4 pm. How did the shadow change during the day?

WHAT HAPPENED?

The shadows are longer when the Sun is low in the sky, in the early morning and late afternoon or evening. The shadow is shortest when the Sun is highest in the sky, at midday.

15 mins

EXPLORING GRAVITY

If you hold a ball in your hand then let it go it will fall downwards. This is because of the force of gravity, which pulls the ball towards the Earth. Do this experiment to find out more about how objects fall.

WHAT DO I NEED?
- selection of objects (e.g. tennis ball, large marble, ping-pong ball, paper plate, toy figure, feather, a winged seed, a shell, a conker, 2 sheets of A4 paper, a lump of modelling clay about the same size as the ping-pong ball)

2

WHAT DO I DO?
1. Look closely at the objects. Predict how each one will fall and land if you drop it.

2. Now test to find out if your predictions are correct.

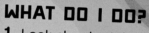

3. Repeat the test on the other objects. Make sure you do the test in the same way to make it a fair test. Keep a record of your results.

4. Do all the objects fall to the ground in the same way? Do some travel more quickly than others? What force do you think is pulling the objects down to the ground? What force slows some objects down?

WHAT HAPPENED?

The balls, the marble, the toy figure, the conker and modelling clay should fall straight down. If you drop any two together, they should hit the ground at the same time. The paper plate, piece of A4 paper, feather and winged seed should have fallen more slowly. That is because their shape allows them to partly float on the air. If there was no air, all the objects would fall at the same speed and hit the ground at the same time. The two balls bounce but not the marble.

When you drop an object, two forces act on it – gravity and air resistance. Air resistance is the force of the air pushing back against a moving object. Gravity pulls an object towards the ground, while air resistance pushes up against it. The larger the surface of the falling object, the greater the air resistance.

5. Screw up one piece of A4 paper into a ball. Predict how you think it will fall. Drop it at the same time as the flat sheet of A4 paper. Do they land at the same time? Why?

6. Make a ball out of the modelling clay (about the same size as the ping-pong ball). Predict how the ping-pong ball and modelling clay will fall and land. Drop them together from the same height. Do they land at the same time?

20 mins

FEEL THE FRICTION

Rub your hands together. Can you feel the palms passing over each other? You are feeling friction. Friction is a type of force. Sometimes it is useful, but sometimes it is not. Find out more in this experiment.

WHAT DO I DO?

1. Hold the skate and push it along a smooth floor surface. What does it feel like? Is it very easy, easy, hard or very hard to push?

WHAT DO I NEED?

- roller-blade (in-line skate)
- skateboard
- different floor surfaces

1

2. Now predict how it will feel to push the skate on four other types of surface, such as a wooden floor, a carpet, a thick rug and tiles.

3. Test to find out if your predictions are correct. Record your results in a table like the one shown below.

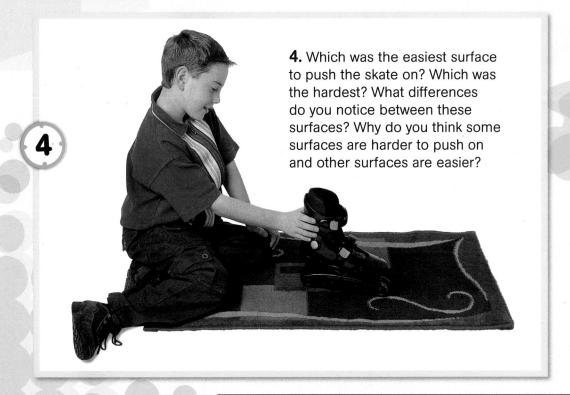

4. Which was the easiest surface to push the skate on? Which was the hardest? What differences do you notice between these surfaces? Why do you think some surfaces are harder to push on and other surfaces are easier?

5. Make a table like the one on the right and fill it in.

type of floor	How did it feel to push the skate?			
	very easy	easy	hard	very hard
wooden floor				
carpet				
thick rug				
tiles				

6. Put the skates on and go outside. Predict which surface will be easiest to skate on and which will be the hardest. Test to see if your predictions are correct. Is the smoothest surface always the easiest to skate on? Is the roughest surface always the hardest?

7. Use a skateboard to move on the same surfaces outside and find out which are easiest and hardest to move on. Were your results the same as with the skates?

WHAT HAPPENED?

Friction occurs when one surface moves across another surface. The smoother the floor, the easier it should have been to push the skate or skateboard.
This is because a smooth surface generates less friction.

SLOW LANDING

30 mins

In the experiment on gravity (pages 82–83) some of the objects fell more slowly because they floated down. Parachutes are designed to drop slowly through the air, but what size and shape makes the best parachute?

WHAT DO I NEED?

- plastic bin liners
- 3 small toy figures of the same weight
- 1 larger toy figure
- ruler
- tape
- strong thread
- scissors
- stopwatch
- a friend
- pencil and paper

WHAT DO I DO?

1. Make three different sized parachutes by first cutting three squares, with sides measuring 20cm, 30cm and 40cm from the plastic bags. These will form the canopies of the parachutes.

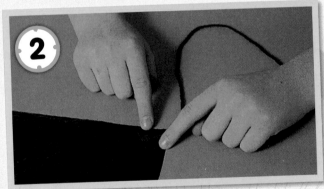

2. Then cut twelve 30-cm lengths of thread and tape a piece to each corner of the plastic squares.

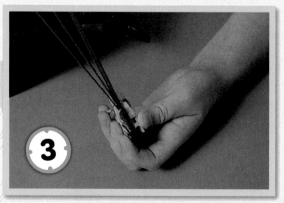

3. On each parachute, tie the four loose ends of thread together then tape to a toy figure.

4. Predict which parachute will be the fastest to travel to the ground and which will be the slowest.

5. Test to find out by standing on a chair or table (make sure an adult holds it steady) and throwing each parachute into the air in the same way each time. Ask a friend to time its journey from dropping to landing with a stopwatch.

⑤

⑤

6. Which parachute took the longest time? Which took the shortest? Why? Which parachute do you think would give the most comfortable journey and safest landing?

7. Make another 40cm square parachute in the same way as before but this time use a larger figure. Compare how this one falls with the 40cm square parachute that has the smaller figure attached.

8. Draw a picture of a parachute falling to the ground. Use arrows to show the direction in which the forces of gravity and air resistance are acting.

WHAT HAPPENED?

The biggest parachute should have taken the longest time to fall. This is because it traps more air and produces more air resistance. Air resistance is the force of the air pushing back against any object moving through it.

MOVING THROUGH WATER

When something moves through water, it is slowed down by water resistance, that is by the water pushing back against it. Make different shaped boats and test which one produces most water resistance and which produces least.

WHAT DO I NEED?

- 3 large rectangular aluminium food trays
- a piece of guttering with end stops about 1m long
- 3 pieces of string or wool just over 75cm long
- aluminium foil
- washers for weights
- sticky tape
- stopwatch
- pencil and paper
- straw
- modelling clay

WHAT DO I DO?

1. First make three 'boats' with different shaped fronts. Fold foil around one tray to make a pointed front and around another to make a curved front. Leave one 'boat' as it is. Predict which boat will be fastest and which will be slowest.

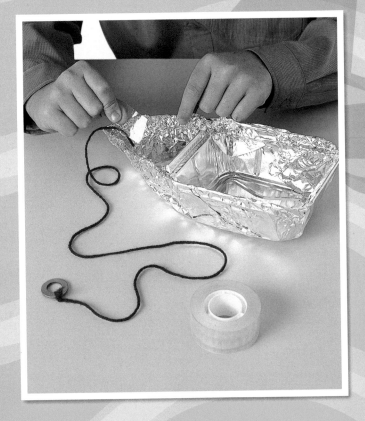

2. Tie a washer onto one end of each piece of string. Tape the other end to the inside front of each boat.

3. Put the guttering on a table with one end at the table's edge or overhanging it. Fill the guttering almost full of water.

4. Now hold one boat at one end of the guttering and hang the washer on the string over the opposite end. Let the boat go, so that the weight of the washer falling pulls it along. Use the stopwatch to time how long it takes the boat to reach the end of the gutter.

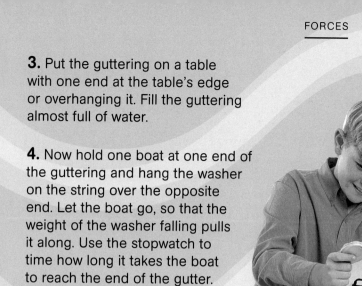

5. Test the other boats in the same way. Which one is fastest? Which one is slowest? Was your prediction correct?

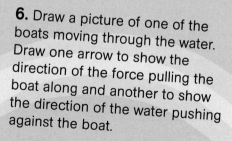

WHAT HAPPENED?

The boat with the pointed front should have been the fastest and the rectangular one the slowest. The pointed one cuts through water (and the air) and so reduces resistance. The rounded boat created less resistance than the rectangular one. That is because it allowed water to flow round it more easily. Engineers design boats, cars and other vehicles to reduce resistance. This is called streamlining.

6. Draw a picture of one of the boats moving through the water. Draw one arrow to show the direction of the force pulling the boat along and another to show the direction of the water pushing against the boat.

7. Try making a sail for each boat out of paper and a straw and stick them in with Blu-tack. Test your boats as before but move them along by blowing with a hand-held fan. Is the same boat fastest now?

20 mins

A LIFTING MACHINE

Machines are designed to help you do things more easily and with less force. A lever is a simple machine that allows you to lift heavy loads more easily. If possible, do this experiment outside!

WHAT DO I DO?

1. Put the ruler on the table so that 20cm of it are touching the table. Place the tin on the end of the ruler on the table.

1

2

2. Hang the bucket on the other end of the ruler.

3. Slowly pour water into the bucket until the tin starts to lift. Don't pour in so much water that the bucket falls off.

3

4. Pour the water from the bucket into the measuring jug and note how much there is. Empty the water back into the first jug.

5. Move the ruler so that 15cm of it are touching the table. Repeat the experiment. Now move the ruler so that only 10cm of it are touching the table and repeat the experiment. What do you notice about the amount of water you need to lift the tin each time?

WHAT HAPPENED?

The less water you need to add to the bucket, the smaller the force needed to lift the tin. You should have found that the least force was needed when the 'handle' of the lever (the part hanging over the table) was longest.

6. Make a graph to show your results.

91

10 mins

MAKE A CATAPULT

In ancient times, armies used catapults, a kind of lever, to attack castles and the people inside them. You can make a simple catapult using a ruler and an eraser.

WHAT DO I NEED?
- ruler
- eraser
- several sheets of A4 paper

WHAT DO I DO?

1. Fold each sheet of paper in half and then in half again lengthwise. Tear along the folds. Fold each strip in half and then in half again. Tear along the folds. Scrunch up each piece of paper to make pellets.

2. Place the ruler over the eraser so that the eraser is at the 8cm mark.

3. Place a pellet at the 30cm mark.

4. Flick the short end down. What happens? Did it go mostly forward or upward? What do you have to do to get the pellet to go farthest?

WHAT HAPPENED?
Flicking down the short end of the lever makes the long end move farther and faster, giving the pellet a bigger push. The more force you use to flick the ruler, the higher the pellet goes. If you want to flick it forward, use less force.

15 mins SEESAWS

A seesaw is a lever that has its pivot at the centre. When the weights at each end are equal, the seesaw remains level and balanced. This experiment uses a seesaw to compare the weights of different objects.

WHAT DO I NEED?

- strong ruler
- chunky eraser
- several small things, such as small toys, stones, wooden blocks

2. Put an object at each end of the ruler. Does the ruler stay balanced, or does one end go down and the other up?

WHAT DO I DO?

1. Balance the ruler on the eraser so that it is level and steady.

3. Which of the objects do you think will be the heaviest and which the lightest? Test them on the ruler. Were you right?

WHAT HAPPENED?

The ruler tilted down on the side of the heavier object. The ruler stayed balanced when the objects on each end were the same weight. The lightest object will never tilt down.

93

GLOSSARY

absorb Soak up

arteries Tubes which take blood from the heart to different parts of the body

attracted Pulled towards

battery A device that generates a small amount of electricity when it is part of a closed circuit

carnivores Animals that eat only meat

circuit A closed loop of electrical components including a battery or other source of electricity

compass An instrument which points to north wherever you are

component A part of a whole

compost Rich soil made by rotting down the remains of plants

condense Change from a gas to a liquid

conductor Something that allows sound, electricity or heat to pass along it

crystal A solid particle with a symmetrical shape made up of several flat surfaces and sharp angles

curdle When substances in a liquid turn into solid lumps

dense How closely packed together the particles that form a substance are

dissolve When a solid breaks up into such tiny pieces in a liquid that it seems to disappear

ear canal The channel that leads from the outer ear to the eardrum

electricity A form of energy which is used to power machines, lights and other things

elliptical Oval-shaped

evaporate Change from a liquid to a gas

food chain A diagram that shows how living things are linked by food

force A push or a pull that affects the way something moves, or changes its shape

freeze Change from a liquid to a solid as a substance becomes cooler

friction The force that is generated when one surface moves over another. Friction acts to slow the movement down

gravity The force that pulls an object towards a larger object, such as Earth

habitat A place where particular types of plants and animals live together

herbivores Animals that eat only plants

insoluble Not able to dissolve in a liquid

insulator Something that stops sound, electricity or heat passing through it

magnetic Able to stick to a magnet

magnify Make larger

melt Change from a solid to a liquid as a substance becomes hotter

motor A device that uses electricity to generate movement

muscles Fleshy parts of the body which move the bones

non-magnetic Not attracted to a magnet

omnivores Animals that eat both plants and meat

opaque Blocking almost all the light

phases (of the Moon) The changing shape of the lit area of the Moon, as seen from Earth

pistil The female part of a flower. New seeds develop at the bottom of the pistil

pivot Point around which a lever moves

planet A large object or ball of gas that moves around the Sun or other star

poles (of a magnet) The parts of a magnet where the magnetic force is strongest. This is usually at the ends

pulse The beats, which are made by the heart pumping blood into the arteries and can be felt in the artery at the wrist and in the neck

reflect Bounce back

resistance A force that acts to slow down movement

roots The parts of a plant that take in water

seedling A small plant

shadow An area that is less well lit than the surrounding area. A shadow is produced when a beam of light is blocked by an object

shoot The first tiny stem and leaves that grow

skeleton All the bones in the body

soluble Able to dissolve in a liquid

solution A liquid which has a substance dissolved in it

sound waves Pattern of movement in a substance as sound passes through it

stalk The part of a plant that joins the roots to the leaves and flowers

stamen The male part of a flower. Stamens produce a fine dust called pollen, which is needed to make new seeds

switch A device for turning a circuit on and off

symbol A drawing or letter which stands for a particular thing

translucent Letting some light through, but not enough to see clearly

transparent Letting almost all the light through

vertebrates Animals with a backbone

vibrate Move forwards and backwards very fast

volume (of sound) how loud or quiet a sound is

water cycle The constant movement of water from the surface of Earth into the air and back to the surface. Water evaporates from oceans, rivers and other wet places into the air. There it condenses to form clouds of water droplets, which join together and fall back to the surface as rain or snow

INDEX